ARTS AND CRAFTS FURNITURE

The Complete Brooks Catalog of 1912

Brooks Manufacturing Co.

A JOINT PUBLICATION OF
THE ATHENAEUM OF PHILADELPHIA
AND
DOVER PUBLICATIONS, INC., NEW YORK

Published in Canada by General Publishing Company, Ltd., 30
Lesmill Road, Don Mills, Toronto, Ontario.
Published in the United Kingdom by Constable and Company, Ltd.,
3 The Lanchesters, 162–164 Fulham Palace Road, London W6 9ER.

This Athenaeum of Philadelphia/Dover edition, first published in
1993, is an unabridged republication of *Brooks Arts and Crafts Furniture
Catalog No. 14*, January 1912, originally published by the Brooks Manufacturing Co., Saginaw, Michigan. The promotional letter, originally a
loose adjunct to the catalog, is here included in the front-matter pages.
The color plate "Stains and Leathers," also loose originally, appears here
on the inside back cover. A new preface and publisher's note have been
added in the present edition.

Manufactured in the United States of America
Dover Publications, Inc., 31 East 2nd Street, Mineola, N.Y. 11501

Library of Congress Cataloging-in-Publication Data

Brooks Manufacturing Co.
    [Brooks arts and crafts furniture. Catalog no. 14]
    Arts and crafts furniture : the complete Brooks catalog of 1912 /
Brooks Manufacturing Co. — 1st Athenaeum of Philadelphia/Dover
ed.
        p.   cm.
    Originally published: Brooks arts and crafts furniture, catalog no.
14. Saginaw, Mich. : Brooks Manufacturing Co., 1912.
    ISBN 0-486-27471-3 (pbk.)
    1. Brooks Manufacturing Co.—Catalogs.   2. Arts and crafts
movement—Michigan—Saginaw—Catalogs.   3. Furniture—
Michigan—Saginaw—History—20th   century—Catalogs.
I. Title.
NK2439.B76A4   1993
684.1′0029′477446—dc20   92-44407
                                                                CIP

PREFACE TO
THE ATHENAEUM/DOVER EDITION

T HIS REPRINT EDITION of the January 1912 catalog of Brooks Arts and Crafts Furniture is one in a series of reprints of books and trade catalogs published by special agreement between The Athenaeum of Philadelphia and Dover Publications, Inc. The objective of this series is to make available to the greatest possible audience rare and often fragile documents from the extensive collections of The Athenaeum in sturdy and inexpensive editions.

The Athenaeum of Philadelphia is an independent research library with museum collections founded in 1814 to collect materials "connected with the history and antiquities of America, and the useful arts, and generally to disseminate useful knowledge." It is housed in a handsomely restored National Historic Landmark building near Independence Hall in the heart of the historic area of Philadelphia.

As the collections expanded over the past 175 years, The Athenaeum refined its objectives. Today the library concentrates on nineteenth- and early twentieth-century social and cultural history, particularly architecture and interior design where the collections are nationally significant. The library is freely open to serious investigators, and it annually attracts thousands of readers: graduate students and senior scholars, architects, interior designers, museum curators and private owners of historic houses.

In addition to 130,000 architectural drawings, 25,000 historic photographs and several million manuscripts, The Athenaeum's library is particularly rich in original works on architecture, interior design and domestic technology. In the latter area the publications of manufacturers and dealers in architectural elements and interior embellishments have been found to be particularly useful to design professionals and historic house owners who are concerned with the restoration or the recreation of period interiors. Consequently, many of the reprints in this series are drawn from this collection. The Athenaeum's holdings are particularly strong in areas such as paint colors, lighting fixtures, wallpaper, heating and kitchen equipment, plumbing and household furniture.

The modern Athenaeum also sponsors a diverse program of lectures, chamber music concerts and exhibitions. It publishes books that reflect the institution's collecting interests, and it administers several trusts that provide awards and research grants to recognize literary achievement and to encourage outstanding scholarship in architectural history throughout the United States. For further information, write The Athenaeum of Philadelphia, East Washington Square, Philadelphia, PA 19106-3794.

ROGER W. MOSS
Executive Director

PUBLISHER'S NOTE

THE ARTS AND CRAFTS movement, established in England by the poet and decorator William Morris, sought to reintroduce the high standards and construction methods of medieval craftsmanship. In the United States the Arts and Crafts movement found expression in the Mission style, which took its inspiration from the hand-crafted wooden furniture created by local artisans in the eighteenth and nineteenth centuries for the Roman Catholic missions in Mexico and the Southwest, which were in turn derived from Spanish domestic furniture designs. The chief proponent of the Mission style in the United States was Gustav Stickley, whose designs, along with those of his brothers, L. and J. G. Stickley, inspired a nationwide enthusiasm for this particular style; their success encouraged many imitators.

The Brooks Manufacturing Co. was established in Saginaw, Michigan, in 1901 and was incorporated in 1903 as the Brooks Boat Manufacturing Company. The company changed its name in 1909 to the Brooks Manufacturing Co. as it became active in the burgeoning Michigan furniture industry. Brooks was one of several manufacturers—such as the Come-Packt Company of Ann Arbor and the Oakcraft Furniture Company of Portland, Michigan—of unassembled yet fully finished furniture, easily put together by the customer, who was assured that "the only tool required is a screwdriver." Brooks's line of tables, chairs, cabinets, bookshelves and other household items was known as Knock-Down (K.D.) furniture, and its manufacture and distribution made possible factory-direct marketing to all parts of the country at substantial discounts over retail show-room prices.

Although the Stickley brothers' influence is evident throughout the Brooks catalog, a number of pieces are reproductions of designs by Charles Limbert. Limbert was a salesman for the John A. Colby Furniture Company of Chicago who in 1889 moved to Grand Rapids, Michigan, where he established his own firm, Charles P. Limbert and Company. The umbrella stand (No. 430) and the tabourette (No. 435) in the present catalog are exact copies of Limbert's designs.

By 1915, the public's interest in the Arts and Crafts movement had waned and the heavy oak Mission style was barely in vogue. Mahogany became the material of choice, which spelled disaster for the oak-based Michigan furniture industry. By the end of the First World War this industry, centered around Grand Rapids—whose name had become synonymous with the production of inexpensive furniture of reliable quality—had declined. Those firms unequipped to move into production of the newer styles soon failed. The Brooks Manufacturing Co. remained in business until August 1922, when it declared bankruptcy.

The inherent irony of this aspect of the American furniture industry lies in the disdain which the Arts and Crafts founder, William Morris, held for machine-driven industry. That his commitment to the ideals of the craftsman and his handiwork, reaffirmed by Gustav Stickley's adherence to those ideals, could only be realized to meet the demands of a mass market by means of mechanical reproduction is a rueful commentary on the economics of supply-and-demand.

The letter from C. A. Herwig, General Sales Manager of the Brooks Manufacturing Co., reproduced in the present volume, accompanied the original catalog and is an interesting example of a contemporary sales "pitch." The inside back cover reproduces a color page, also sent with the original catalog, showing the various custom finishes available.

BROOKS MANUFACTURING CO,

C. A. Herwig,
    General Sales Manager,

                                        Saginaw, Mich.

    My Dear Friend:—

        Your appreciated inquiry in response
to our advertisement shows that you have some
idea of the tremendous money-saving possi-
bilities of buying our K.D. Furniture direct
from the factory.

        I thank you for your inquiry and take
pleasure in enclosing herewith a copy of
our latest catalog of K.D., quarter-sawed,
solid oak Mission Furniture. Am mighty en-
thusiastic over this knock-down furniture,
knowing from the business of the past year
that we have the best proposition on the
market today from the buyer's point of view.

        In addition to furnishing quarter-sawed
oak, I want to say that we have reduced our
prices way below any previous catalog issued.
Now, I must ask your assistance in maintaining
these low prices as this can only be done by
the doubling of our furniture business. No
furniture factory in the world today can com-
pete with us on the bargains offered in this
catalog—and furnish the same high-grade of
solid oak, quarter-sawed furniture. I know it—
positively—and you can convince yourself by
simply comparing our prices with those of your
local dealer. You will at once appreciate the

great saving that can be effected by purchasing our furniture in the finished sections, simply putting it together as explained in ''Our Proposition'' on page one of Catalog.

To be candid with you, I am mighty anxious for you to get started with us. I want you to send me a trial order and be convinced that I can save you money. I know absolutely that if I can get you to give me a trial order you will become a regular customer and will take great pleasure in recommending us to your friends and neighbors.

Fill out the enclosed trial order blank— right now—while you think of it. This blank gives you the right to return the furniture if it does not meet with your entire satisfaction and far exceed your expectations. That removes the risk. It makes you the sole judge of the proposition. You cannot lose.

Study dimensions—make comparisons, but for our sake be careful. Some of the pieces are too massive for small rooms. Remember, we have to pay for your mistakes.

You will note we are also listing a line of wicker furniture, together with Rugs, Mission lamps, lace curtains, kitchen cabinets, vacuum cleaners, fireless cookers, etc. We do not manufacture these articles but through close affiliations with the manufacturers, are in a position to list them at a less cost than you could obtain locally. Appreciating the increased demand for same, we list them as a special proposition.

If you are interested in the practical dollar-saving side of purchasing your furniture, you cannot afford to overlook this exceptional offer. The time to act is now. Money is not saved by those who hesitate. It is saved by those who have the power of decision—to take action without delay. A dollar saved is a dollar made.

Here is your opportunity. Fill out the enclosed trial order blank and mail it to me today—DO IT NOW.

Very cordially yours,

BROOKS MANUFACTURING CO.,

C. A. Strong

CAH/BES   General Sales Manager.

P. S.—Be sure and read ''Modern Purchasing'' on page two, also ''Description of Material'' on page four of catalog.

BR8KS FURNITURE

[original front cover]

BROOKS
ARTS and CRAFTS
FURNITURE

Catalog № 14
January 1912

Superseding all
Previous Catalogs

Our Proposition

TO place in your home high grade, solid quarter sawed oak furniture—furniture that lends a tone of elegance, of distinction, to any room, honest furniture that will pass down to generations—at a cost that is ridiculously low. This is our proposition. How? By our supplying finished sections, ready to assemble, so that they can be shipped direct to you in a compact box, you simply putting the joints together in the grooves provided, thereby eliminating the numerous margins of profit that keep adding to the selling price of any commodity in its long routine from the producer to the consumer.

The work of putting the sections together is simple. It can be done by any woman. No skill or special knowledge is required. There are no holes to bore—no sawing—no tool work. The only tool required is a screwdriver.

OUR GUARANTEE—We absolutely guarantee that you will be satisfied with everything you purchase of us or we will instantly refund every penny you have paid us. Please note— This doesn't mean simply that we guarantee against defective workmanship and material or that we guarantee goods to be as represented—it means satisfaction—your satisfaction—you to be the judge and decide—your decision to be final without question or quibble on our part.

OUR REFERENCES—As to our responsibility, we refer you to the Second National Bank of Saginaw, or to the Commercial Agencies.

BROOKS MANUFACTURING CO.

Saginaw, Michigan, U. S. A.

Established 1901   Capital Stock $400,000.00

C. C. BROOKS, President   F. G. PALMERTON, Vice-President   J. O. PIERCE, Secretary and Treasurer

The Originators of the Knock-Down System of Home Furnishing

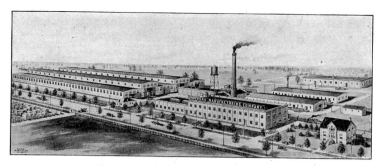

The largest plant of its kind in the world. Occupying Fifteen Acres of Ground and Five Acres of Floor Space

Modern Purchasing

BUYING goods by mail, heretofore generally misunderstood but now better recognized as "Modern Purchasing" offers, beyond a question of a doubt the greatest opportunity for money saving in the business world today.

It is a well recognized fact that the business methods of the country are undergoing a process of evolution, gradual to be sure, but nevertheless as absolutely certain.

The old method of selling any manufactured product, consisted in locating the dealer—not the consumer—demonstrating the goods to be disposed of, indulging in extended talks and expense, and convincing the retailer that the demand for the goods would justify his adding a margin, over and above the cost to him, sufficient to cover the proper proportion of his operating expenses and profit, and finally effecting a sale. All of which added substantially to the cost of the consumer, but not to the value of the goods.

The modern way is for the producer to talk direct by mail, to a thousand prospective consumers at one time, and effecting sales without seeing any of them. Consider the saving to the consumer. Figure it out yourself.

From the best information obtainable, the buying public can be divided as follows:

Five per cent buy the highest priced merchandise, in the belief that the more they pay the better the goods.

Ten per cent buy the cheapest, regardless of quality.

Eighty-five per cent buy the best at the lowest price.

In buying by mail the consumer takes no risk for it is imperative that, in order to establish a business integrity, a business that insures permanency, the manufacturer stands back of his goods with a guarantee of satisfaction or money refunded. Such a policy necessarily precludes the marketing of misrepresented or inferior goods—they must be standard in every respect. The purchaser does not risk one cent. The manufacturer, if reliable, is rated in the recognized Commercial Agencies, which rating, if doubted, can be ascertained by inquiring at any bank in the United States. His financial standing and business integrity depends absolutely on the sincerity of his guarantee. Over and above this, the permanency of his business depends strictly on his advertised guarantee. Why? Because the reputable publications of the day will not accept advertisements from any manufacturer unless his business integrity is such that the publishers, personally, can stand back of every statement.

As the world advances, the buying public is awakening to the fact that the closer the contact of the consumer with the producer, the greater amount of saving to be effected.

The thinking man asks himself why he should pay so many middle profits—why, in addition to the actual manufacturing cost, with the proper proportion added for factory, office expenses and profit, should he be compelled to pay for the maintenance of an expensive force of traveling salesmen to reach the dealer, the dealer's expense and profit thereby practically doubling the cost to the consumer without adding one cent's actual value to the product. Think it over and the appeal of the local dealer to **keep your money at home** will immediately have a literal significance. You will decide to do so but it will be to keep it in your **own** home where **you, yourself** and **your family** will enjoy the full value of its earning capacity.

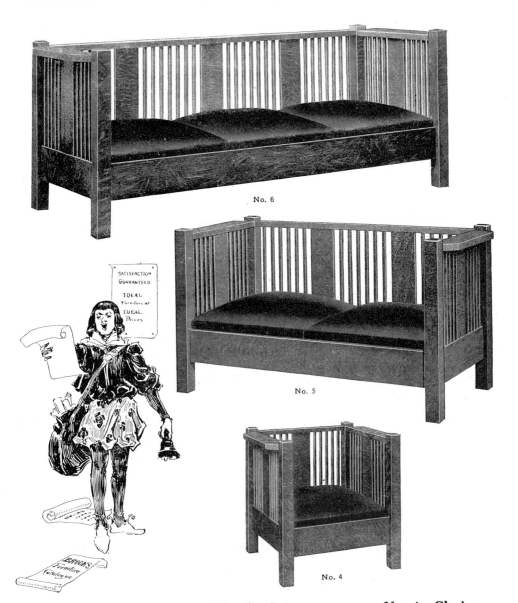

No. 6

No. 5

No. 4

No. 6—Davenport
Brooks Price,
Quartered Oak, $20.25

Dealers Price, $45.00

Height, 35 inches. Depth, 30½ inches.
Length, 88 inches. Shipping weight,
240 lbs.
  Price includes cushions covered with
marokene leather. For genuine leather,
add $7.50.
  No extra charge for one piece cushion,
if desired.

No. 5—Settee
Brooks Price,
Quartered Oak, $14.25

Dealers Price, $35.00

Height, 35 inches. Depth, 30½ inches.
Length, 62 inches. Shipping weight
200 lbs.
  Price includes cushions covered with
marokene leather. For genuine leather,
add $5.00.
  No extra charge for one piece cushion,
if desired.

No. 4--Chair
Brooks Price,
Quartered Oak, $8.25

Dealers Price, $17.50

Height, 35 inches. Depth, 30½ inches.
Width, 36 inches. Shipping weight,
130 lbs.
  Price includes cushions covered with
marokene leather. For genuine leather,
add $2.50.

No. 3

No. 2

No. 01

"A Davenport is most useful where large space must be utilized. Particularly is this true for the furnishing of the Halls. It makes an ideal window seat.

"Settee" is an old fashioned word and it gives old fashioned comfort. A seat for two before a log fire. Most suggestive of "Home."

No. 3—Davenport
Brooks Price,
Quartered Oak, $18.25
Dealers Price, $40.00

Height, 35 inches. Depth, 31 inches Length, 84½ inches. Shipping weight, 220 lbs.
Price includes cushion covered with marokene leather. For genuine leather add $7.50.
No extra charge for one piece cushion, if desired.

No. 01—Chair
Brooks Price,
Quartered Oak, $7.25
Dealers Price, $15.00

Height, 35 inches. Depth, 31 inches. Width, 32½ inches. Shipping weight, 110 lbs.
Price includes cushion covered with marokene leather. For genuine leather, add $2.50.

No. 2—Settee
Brooks Price,
Quartered Oak, $12.75
Dealers Price, $27.00

Height, 35 inches. Depth, 31 inches. Length, 57½ inches. Shipping weight, 160 lbs.
Price includes cushion covered with marokene leather. For genuine leather add $5.00.
No extra charge for one piece cushion, if desired.

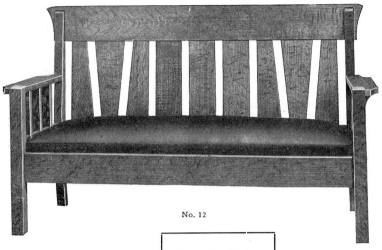

No. 12

> *One splendid fea-
> ture about Brooks
> furniture is that
> pieces of a "set"
> match perfectly, yet
> they are "odd"
> enough to be used
> "singly" with ad-
> vantage.*

No. 11

No 10

No. 11—Chair
Brooks Price,
Quartered Oak, $6.75

Dealers Price, $14.00

Height, 37½ inches. Width, 31 inches. Depth, 21 inches. Shipping weight, 100 lbs.

Price includes cushion covered with marokene leather. For genuine leather, add $2.00.

No. 12—Settee
Brooks Price,
Quartered Oak, $11.75

Dealers Price, $25.00

Height, 37½ inches. Depth, 21 inches. Length, 67 inches. Shipping weight 160 lbs.

Price includes cushion covered with marokene leather. For genuine leather, add $3.50.

No. 10—Rocker
Brooks Price,
Quartered Oak, $7.50

Dealers Price, $16.00

Height, 35 inches. Width, 31 inches. Depth, 21 inches. Shipping weight, 100 lbs.

Price includes cushion covered with marokene leather. For genuine leather, add $2.00.

No. 8

No. 7

*O*ur designer has here combined the famous chippendale effect with the solidity of the "Craftsman" usefulness.

*G*ood taste never varies, it is simply a question of which pleases you the most.

No. 9

No. 8—Chair
Brooks Price,
Quartered Oak, $5.00
Dealers Price, $11.50

Height, 38 inches. Width, 22 inches. Depth, 20 inches. Shipping weight, 80 lbs.
Price includes seat covered with marokene leather. For genuine leather, add $1.00.

No. 9—Settee
Brooks Price,
Quartered Oak, $9.50
Dealers Price, $20.00

Height, 38 inches. Depth, 20 inches. Length, 45 inches. Shipping weight, 100 lbs.
Price includes seat covered with marokene leather. For genuine leather, add $2.00.

No. 7—Rocker
Brooks Price,
Quartered Oak, $5.50
Dealers Price, $13.00

Height, 36 inches. Width, 22 inches. Depth, 20 inches. Shipping weight, 80 lbs.
Price includes seat covered with marokene leather. For genuine leather, add $1.00.

No. 709

Highly ornamental yet possessing a certain in-built dignity.

No. 708

No. 707

No. 708—Chair
Brooks Price, Quartered Oak, $9.25

Dealers Price, $20.00

Height, 37½ inches. Width, 31 inches Depth, 21½ inches. Shipping weight 110 lbs.

Price includes cushion and back panel covered with marokene leather. For genuine leather, add $2.50.

No. 709—Settee
Brooks Price, Quartered Oak, $17.00

Dealers Price, $40.00

Height, 37½ inches. Depth, 21½ inches. Length, 67 inches. Shipping weight, 170 lbs.

Price includes cushion and back panels covered with marokene leather. For genuine leather, add $5.50.

No. 707—Rocker
Brooks Price, Quartered Oak, $10.00

Dealers Price, $22.00

Height, 35 inches. Width, 31 inches. Depth, 21½ inches. Shipping weight, 110 lbs.

Price includes cushion and back panel covered with marokene leather For genuine leather, add $2.50.

No. 28

No. 29

No. 31

No. 30

No. 28—Rocker

Brooks Price,
Quartered Oak, $8.50

Dealers Price, $18.00

Height, 37 inches. Width, 30 inches. Depth, 24 inches. Shipping weight, 100 lbs.

Price includes cushion and back panel covered with maro-kene leather. For genuine leather, add $2.50.

No. 29—Chair

Brooks Price,
Quartered Oak, $7.75

Dealers Price, $16.50

Height, 37 inches. Width, 30 inches. Depth, 24 inches. Shipping weight, 100 lbs.

Price includes cushion and back panel covered with maro-kene leather. For genuine leather, add $2.50.

No. 31—Rocker

Brooks Price,
Quartered Oak, $7.50

Dealers Price, $16.00

Height, 37 inches. Width, 30 inches. Depth, 24 inches. Shipping weight, 100 lbs.

Price includes cushion covered with marokene leather. For genuine leather, add $2.00.

No. 30—Chair

Brooks Price,
Quartered Oak, $6.75

Dealers Price, $15.00

Height, 38½ inches. Width, 30 inches. Depth, 24 inches. Shipping weight, 100 lbs.

Price includes cushion covered with marokene leather. For genuine leather, add $2.00.

No. 26

No. 27

No. 33

No. 32

No. 26—Chair

Brooks Price,
Quartered Oak, $7.75

Dealers Price, $16.50

Height, 41 inches. Width, 30 inches. Depth, 22 inches. Shipping weight, 100 lbs.
Price includes cushion covered with marokene leather. For genuine leather, add $2.00.

No. 27—Rocker

Brooks Price,
Quartered Oak, $8.50

Dealers Price, $18.00

Height, 40 inches. Width, 30 inches. Depth, 22 inches. Shipping weight, 100 lbs.
Price includes cushion covered with marokene leather For genuine leather, add $2.00.

No. 33—Chair

Brooks Price,
Quartered Oak, $8.75

Dealers Price, $19.00

Height, 44½ inches. Depth, 24 inches. Width, 30 inches. Shipping weight, 100 lbs.
Price includes cushion and back panel covered with marokene leather. For genuine leather, add $3.00.

No. 32—Rocker

Brooks Price,
Quartered Oak, $9.50

Dealers Price, $20.00

Height, 43 inches. Depth, 24 inches. Width, 30 inches. Shipping weight, 100 lbs.
Price includes cushion and back panel covered with maro- kene leather. For genuine leather, add $3.00.

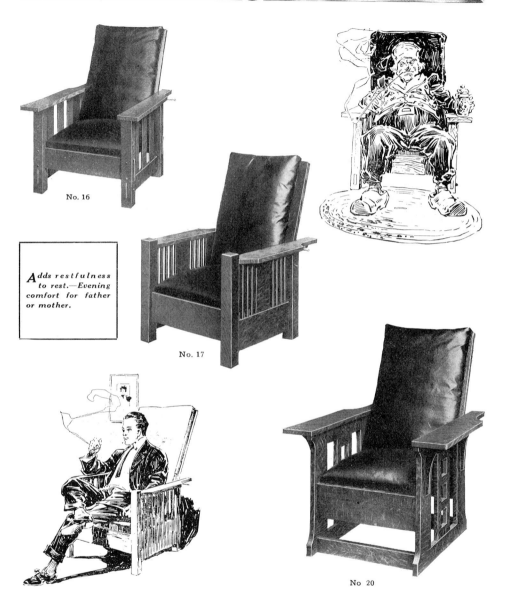

No. 16

Adds restfulness to rest.—Evening comfort for father or mother.

No. 17

No 20

No. 16—Morris Chair

Brooks Price, Quartered Oak, $10.75

Dealers Price, $25.00

Height, 46½ inches. Width, 33 inches, Depth, 37 inches. Shipping weight. 140 lbs.

Price includes cushion and back pillow complete covered with marokene leather. For genuine leather, add $6.50.

No. 17—Morris Chair

Brooks Price, Quartered Oak, $11.75

Dealers Price, $27.50

Height, 46½ inches. Width, 33 inches. Depth, 36 inches. Shipping weight 140 lbs.

Price includes cushion and back pillow complete covered with marokene leather. For genuine leather, add $6.50.

No. 20—Morris Chair

Brooks Price, Quartered Oak, $13.50

Dealers Price, $30.00

Height, 44 inches. Width, 35 inches. Depth, 37 inches. Shipping weight 170 lbs.

Price includes cushion and back pil low complete covered with marokene leather. For genuine leather, add $6.50

No. 1

No. 04

No. 424

No. 422

No. 1—Chair

Brooks Price,
Quartered Oak, $6.75

Dealers Price, $14.00

Height, 35 inches. Width, 28 inches. Depth, 27 inches. Shipping weight, 100 lbs.
Price includes cushion covered with marokene leather. For genuine leather, add $2.00.

No. 424—Foot Stool

Brooks Price,
Quartered Oak, $2.00

Dealers Price, $5.00

Height, 9 inches. Depth, 12 inches. Length, 18 inches. Shipping weight, 40 lbs.
Price includes top covered with marokene leather. For genuine leather, add $1.50.

No. 04—Chair

Brooks Price,
Quartered Oak, $7.25

Dealers Price, $16.00

Height, 35 inches. Width, 28 inches. Depth, 27 inches. Shipping weight, 100 lbs.
Price includes cushion covered with marokene leather. For genuine leather, add $2.00.

No. 422—Foot Rest

Brooks Price,
Quartered Oak, $3.50

Dealers Price, $7.50

Height, 17 inches. Depth, 14 inches. Length, 27 inches. Shipping weight, 40 lbs.
Price includes cushion covered with marokene leather. For genuine leather, add $2.00.

No. 310

No. 14

No. 310—Extension Dining Table

Brooks Price,
Quartered Oak, $13.00

Dealers Price, $28.00

Height, 30 inches. Top, closed 48 inches square. Top, extended, 48 x 84 inches. Shipping weight, 220 lbs. Three leaves furnished with each table.

No. 14—Dining Chair

Brooks Price,
Quartered Oak, { Set of Four $ 9.00
{ Set of Six 13.25

Dealers Price, Set of Six, $21.00

Height, 39 inches. Depth, 18 inches. Width, 17½ inches. Shipping weight, (4) 140 lbs.; (6) 170 lbs.

Price includes seat covered with marokene leather. For genuine leather, add, for four, $3.75; for six, $5.50.

> When in use, a hospitable Board for family and friendly gatherings. When not in use, a piece of furniture worthy any home. Artistic chairs to match— Note the prices.

No. 312

No. 18

No. 312—Breakfast Table

Brooks Price,
Quartered Oak, $9.00

Dealers Price, $20.00

Height, 30 inches. Top, 42 inches. Solid Top, does not extend. Shipping weight, 140 lbs.

This table also makes an ideal round top center or card table.

No. 18—Dining Chair
Brooks Price,

	One	$2.00
Quartered Oak,	Set of Four	7.50
	Set of Six	11.00

Dealers Price, Set of Six, $21.00

Height, 43 inches. Width at back, 13 inches. Depth, 17 inches. Shipping weight (4), 100 lbs.; (5) 150 lbs.

Price quoted is for solid seat only.

No. 311

No. 13

> *"Let good diges-tion wait on appe-tite."* Good things to eat presuppose a good dining room suite. Good furni-ture does not always imply costliness as the prices of Brooks furniture more than proves.

No. 15

No. 13—Dining Chair

Brooks Price, Quartered Oak,
Set of Four $ 9.50
Set of Six   14.00

Dealers Price, Set of Six, $24 00

Height, 39 inches. Width, 17½ inches. Depth, 18 inches. Shipping weight, (4) 140 lbs.; (6) 170 lbs.
Price includes seat covered with marokene leather. For genuine leather, add, for four, $3.75; for six, $5.50.

No. 311—Extension Dining Table

Brooks Price, Quartered Oak, $19.00

Dealers Price, $45.00

Height, 30 inches. Top closed, 54 inches. Top Extended, 90 inches. Shipping weight, 300 lbs.
Three leaves furnished with each table.

No. 15—Dining Chair

Brooks Price, Quartered Oak,
Set of Four $11.50
Set of Six   16.50

Dealers Price, Set of Six, $30.00

Height, 39 inches. Width, 17½ inches. Depth, 18 inches. Shipping weight, (4) 140 lbs; (6) 170 lbs.
Price includes seat and back panel covered with marokene leather. For genuine leather, add, for four, $5.50: for six, $8.00.

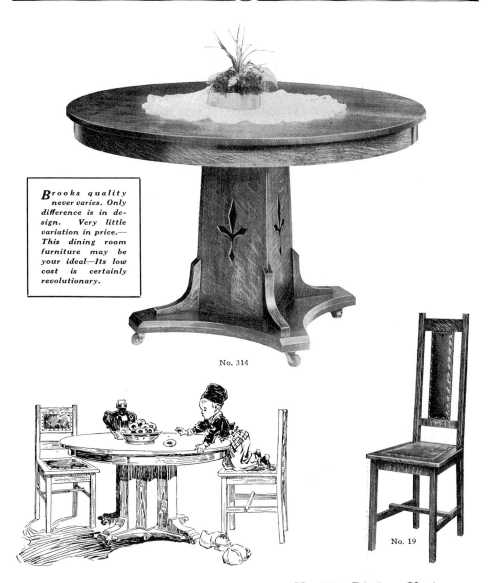

Brooks quality never varies. Only difference is in design. Very little variation in price.— This dining room furniture may be your ideal.—Its low cost is certainly revolutionary.

No. 314

No. 19

No. 314—Extension Dining Table

Brooks Price,
Quartered Oak, $15.50

Dealers Price, $35.00

Height, 30 inches. Top closed, 48 inches. Top extended, 72 inches. Pedestal, 10 inches square at bottom, 8½ inches square at top. Shipping weight, 230 lbs.

Two leaves furnished with each table.

No. 19—Dining Chair

Brooks Price,

Quartered Oak,
One	$ 2.75
Set of Four	10.00
Set of Six	14.50

Dealers Price, Set of Six, $24.00

Height, 43 inches. Depth, 17 inches. Width at back, 13 inches. Shipping weight (4), 100 lbs.; (6) 150 lbs.

Price includes seat and back panel covered with marokene leather. For genuine leather, add, for (1) $1.00; for (4) $4.00. for (6) $5.50.

Both Nos. 18 and 19 individually can be used to advantage as reception chairs or in connection with our writing desks.

No. 711

If we sold furniture by looks we could ask twice the price and every purchaser would still own a bargain.

No. 713

No. 715

No. 713—Dining Chair

Brooks Price, Quartered Oak,

Set of Four	. .	$15.00
Set of Six	. .	22.00

Dealers Price, $8.00 each

Height, 39 inches. Width, 17½ inches. Depth, 18 inches. Shipping weight, (4) 150 lbs.; (6) 190 lbs.
Price includes seat and back panel covered with marokene leather. For genuine leather, add for four, $5.00; for six, $7.50.

No. 711—Extension Dining Table

Brooks Price, Quartered Oak, $21.50

Dealers Price, $50.00

Height, 30 inches. Top closed, 54 inches. Table extended, 90 inches. Shipping weight, 300 lbs.
Three leaves furnished with each table.

No. 715—Arm Dining Chair

Brooks Price, Quartered Oak,

One	. . . .	$ 5.00
Set of Four	. .	19.00
Set of Six .	. .	28.00

Dealers Price, $11.00 each

Height, 39 inches. Width, 25 inches. Depth, 18 inches. Shipping weight, (1) 60 lbs.; (4) 190 lbs.; (6) 230 lbs.
Price includes seat and back panel covered with marokene leather. For genuine leather, add, for one $1.50; for four, $6.00; for six, $9.00.

No. 710

> *Here is a challenge in beauty, a challenge in workmanship, a challenge in value. An ornament to any home. A luxury and a necessity.*

No. 710—Buffet

Brooks Price,
Quartered Oak, $27.00

Dealers Price, $60.00

Height, 52 inches. Depth, 19 inches. Length, 55 inches. Shipping weight, 250 lbs.

We will furnish oak panels for doors in place of glass if desired. The mirror furnished is of the best bevelled plate.

No. 410

There is a chaste dignity about this "piece" that is rich without being ornate, and a joy to the eye. Note the grain of the wood—and the price.

No. 410—Buffet

Brooks Price, Quartered Oak, $25.00

Dealers Price, $55.00

Height, 51 inches. Depth, 19 inches. Length, 55 inches. Shipping weight, 280 lbs.

We will furnish oak panels for doors in place of glass, if desired. The mirror furnished is of the best bevelled plate.

No 411

There's something about this Buffet that takes us back over the years.—Our ancestors made furniture strong yet simple in design—we believe that is the distinctive charm of this piece. Don't you?

No. 411—Buffet

Brooks Price,
Quartered Oak, $17.00

Dealers Price, $35.00

Height, 49 inches.   Depth, 18 inches.   Length, 55 inches.
Shipping weight, 260 lbs.

No 720

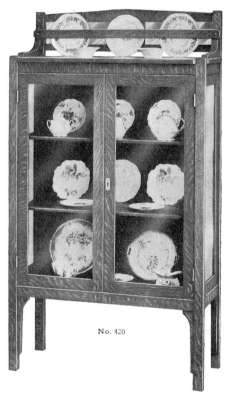

No. 420

No. 720—China Closet

Brooks Price,
Quartered Oak, $18.50

Dealers Price, $40.00

Height, 61 inches. Width, 36 inches. Depth, 15 inches. Shipping weight, 200 lbs.
Price includes glass inserted. Mirror furnished is of the best bevelled plate.

No 420—China Closet

Brooks Price,
Quartered Oak, $16.50

Dealers Price, $35.00

Height, 61 inches. Width, 36 inches. Depth, 15 inches. Shipping weight, 200 lbs.
Price includes glass inserted.

No. 426

> *Good furniture is meant to beautify but one must include its usefulness when deciding its purchase. Here are two pieces that are ideal for library or den. Good to look at and decidedly useful.*

No. 425

No. 426—Combination Writing Desk

Brooks Price, Quartered Oak, $21.50

Dealers Price, $50.00

Height, 50 inches. Depth, 15 inches. Width, 63 inches. Shipping weight, 250 lbs.
Price includes glass inserted.
Interior of desk compartment fitted with convenient pigeon holes.

No. 425—Writing Desk

Brooks Price, Quartered Oak, $10.50

Dealers Price, $25.00

Height, 50 inches. Depth, 17 inches. Width, 34 inches. Shipping weight, 100 lbs.
Interior of desk arranged with shelves and compartments for writing material, etc.

No. 306

No. 307

No. 307—Center Table

Brooks Price,
Quartered Oak, $8.00

Dealers Price, $18.00

Height, 30 inches. Top, 34 inches in diameter. Shipping weight, 80 lbs.

Price includes top covered with marokene leather and fastened with oxidized tacks. For genuine leather, add $3.00.

No. 306—Library Table

Brooks Price,
Quartered Oak, $15.00

Dealers Price, $35.00

Height, 30 inches. Width, 34 inches. Length, 48 inches. Shipping weight, 160 lbs.

No. 308

A living room is most liveable with an artistic craftsman library table in it. Where you will find the lure of a good book and many a pleasant hour leaning upon its beautifully grained surface.

We know these two Brooks library tables cannot be duplicated in low price, the quality we will leave to your good judgment.

No. 309

No. 308—Library Table

Brooks Price,
Quartered Oak, $10.50

Dealers Price, $25.00

Height, 30 inches. Width, 28 inches. Length, 43 inches.
Shipping weight, 140 lbs.

No. 309—Library Table

Brooks Price,
Quartered Oak, $9.50

Dealers Price, $20.00

Height, 30 inches. Width, 28 inches. Length, 43 inches.
Shipping weight, 120 lbs.

No. 701

No. 300

One distinction about Brooks Furniture is the many varieties of design but a uniform high quality.

No. 701—Library Table

Brooks Price,
Quartered Oak, $13.00

Dealers Price, $30.00

Height, 30 inches. Length, 43 inches. Width, 28 inches. **Shipping** weight, 160 lbs.

No. 300—Center Table

Brooks Price,
Quartered Oak, $4.50

Dealers Price, $9.00

Height, 30 inches. Top, 25 inches square. Shipping weight, 60 lbs.

No. 431

Most business-like, yet decorative.   Adds dignity
to any office.

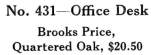

No. 432

No. 431—Office Desk

Brooks Price,
Quartered Oak, $20.50

Dealers Price, $50.00

Height, 30 inches. Depth, 36 inches. Length, 60 inches.
Shipping weight, 330 lbs.

No. 432—Revolving Chair

Brooks Price,
Quartered Oak, $7.00

Dealers Price, $15.00

Height, 36 inches. Width, 24 inches. Depth, 20 inches.
Shipping weight, 90 lbs.
Price includes cushion covered with marokene leather. For
genuine leather, add $2.00.

No. 406

No. 405

No. 438

No. 405—Book Rack
**Brooks Price,
Quartered Oak, $5.00**

Dealers Price, $11.00

Height, 56 inches. Width, 41 inches. Depth, 12 inches. Shipping weight, 80 lbs.

No. 406—Book Case
**Brooks Price,
Quartered Oak, $12.75**

Dealers Price, $28.00

Height, 53½ inches. Width, 36 inches. Depth, 15 inches. Shipping weight, 190 lbs.
Price includes glass inserted.

No. 438—Magazine Rack
**Brooks Price,
Quartered Oak, $4.50**

Dealers Price, $10.00

Height, 40 inches. Depth, 14 inches. Width, 30 inches. Shipping weight, 70 lbs.

No. 413

No. 427

> *"Time is money"* and no money can be spent more economically to always possess the right time in the house, than to own a Brooks Hall Clock.

No. 413—Hall Clock

Brooks Price, Quartered Oak, $18.75

Dealers Price, $40.00

Height, 75 inches. Width, 18 inches. Depth, 14 inches. Shipping weight, 140 lbs.

Fitted with an eight-day weight strike movement on mission gong. Wood rod and brass pendulum ball. Brass numerals and hands.

No. 427—Hall Tree

Brooks Price, Quartered Oak, $7.50

Dealers Price, $17.00

Height, 70 inches. Width, 26 inches. Mirror, 10x12 inches. Shipping weight, 80 lbs.

If tree is to be placed against wall rear portion of base can be removed.

No. 428

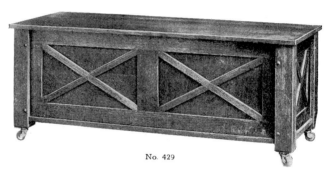

A mirror to look in, a rack to hang garments upon, and a beautiful chest to hold shirt waists, children's clothes, or many other things—what are more useful?

No. 429

No. 428—Hall Mirror

Brooks Price,
Quartered Oak, $6.50

Dealers Price, $14.00

Height, 29 inches. Length, 55 inches. Mirror, **18x20** inches. Shipping weight, 60 lbs.

The mirror furnished is of the best bevelled **plate.**

No. 429—Hall Chest

Brooks Price,
Quartered Oak, $7.50

Dealers Price, $16.00

Height, 20 inches. Width, 20 inches. **Length,** 47 inches. Shipping weight, 100 lbs.

No. 421

No. 433

No. 421—Fern Stand

Brooks Price, Quartered Oak, $2.50

Dealers Price, $6.00

Height, 30 inches. Top, 16 inches square. Shipping weight, 40 lbs. This piece makes an excellent telephone stand.

No. 433—Cellarette

Brooks Price, Quartered Oak, $4.50

Dealers Price, $10.00

Height, 34 inches. Top, 19 inches square. Shipping weight, 60 lbs.

Here are four pieces of real furniture, designed for four entirely different purposes, at an average price of three dollars and a quarter. Most useful, most economical.

No. 430

No. 435

No. 430—Umbrella Stand

Brooks Price, Quartered Oak, $3.00

Dealers Price, $7.00

Height, 28 inches. Base, 15 inches square. Shipping weight, 40 lbs. Price includes pan for base of stand.

No. 435—Tabourette

Brooks Price, Quartered Oak, $3.00

Dealers Price, $7.00

Height, 27 inches. Top, 16 inches each way. Shipping weight, 60 lbs.

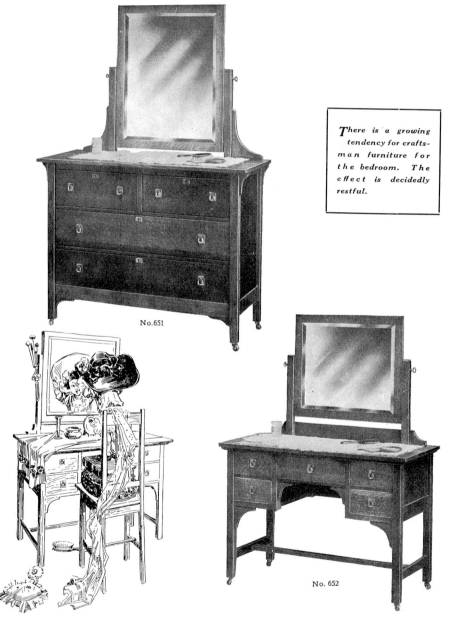

No.651

No. 652

> There is a growing tendency for craftsman furniture for the bedroom. The effect is decidedly restful.

No. 651—Dresser
Brooks Price, Quartered Oak, $15.00
Dealers Price, $35.00

Top, 22x50 inches.   Height, 72 inches.   Shipping weight 260 lbs.
The mirror furnished is of the best bevelled plate, 24x30 inches.

No. 652—Dresser
Brooks Price, Quartered Oak, $13.00
Dealers Price, $30.00

Top, 21½x45 inches.   Height, 59 inches.   Shipping weight 225 lbs.
The mirror furnished is of the best bevelled plate 20x24 inches.

IT is a difficult matter to impart to a prospective customer in a catalog the superior quality, the excellent workmanship, the exquisite solid quarter sawed oak that makes Brooks Furniture the "most talked about" and "the most BOUGHT," factory furniture in the world.

In selling direct to you our only salesman is our catalog. Catalogs are expensive when using the thousands that we do. Consequently, we must be careful of this expensive item as our highest ambition is to make Brooks Furniture superior in quality and lower in price, than any other furniture on the market today. We could put out a catalog that would illustrate all of our furniture as below, but the expense would be enormous, so we are putting this saving into better furniture for our patrons.

For description and price of this rocker see page 7.

"Dost Thou Like

The Furniture in this living room

Table, No. 308	$10.50
Cellarette, No. 433	4.50

Portable Lamp, No. 416L	$ 6.50
Desk, No. 426	21.50

he Picture?'' —*Claude Melnotte*

ll Brooks' Designs will cost $74.25

Foot Rest, No. 422	$3.50	Morris Chair, No. 20	$13.50
Chair, No. 1	6.75	Rocker, No. 31	7.50

VEN this high grade lithographed illlustration does not bring out to advantage the artistic beauty of our solid oak quarter sawed Craftsman Furniture. It is quite impossible to demonstrate by means of a lithographic reproduction the true beauty of the wood as it actually appears in our product, the skilled judgment exercised in the distribution of the material avoids an exaggerated and flashy appearance. On this particular point we specialize, thereby producing the rich and refined appearance characteristic of the Brooks Arts and Crafts Furniture.

For description and price of this table see page No. 17.

Brass Beds tar-nish, cost a lot of money—and are now out of fashion. The Brooks Solid Quartered Oak Bed-steads match the rest of our Bedroom Furniture and are distinctly superior to all other Bed-steads in wearing qualities, simplicity, and in low price.

No. 601

No. 600

No. 600—Bedstead
Brooks Price,
Quartered Oak, $14.50
Dealers Price, $30.00

Height, 54 inches. Width, 54 inches. Length, 78 inches. Shipping weight, 240 lbs.

Note—This bed is also furnished 42 inches wide. Brooks price, Quartered Oak, $12.50. Shipping weight, 200 lbs.

No. 601—Bedstead
Brooks Price,
Quartered Oak, $15.50
Dealers Price, $35.00

Height, 54 inches. Width, 54 inches. Length, 78 inches. Shipping weight, 240 lbs.

Note—This bed is also furnished 42 inches wide. Brooks price, Quartered Oak, $13.50. Shipping weight, 190 lbs.

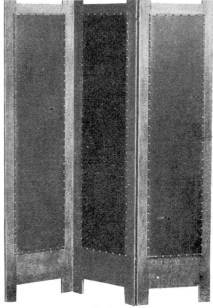

No. 434

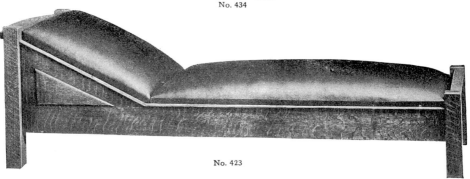

No. 423

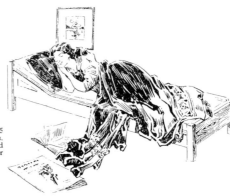

No. 423—Den Couch

Brooks Price, Quartered Oak, $17.00

Dealers Price, $38.00

Width, 31 inches. Length, 85 inches. Shipping weight, 190 lbs. Price includes cushions covered with marokene leather. For genuine leather, add $10.00.

No. 434—Screen

Brooks Price, Quartered Oak, $10.50 Additional Sections $3.50 Each

Height, 72 inches. Width of each section 19 inches. Shipping weight (three sections), 90 lbs.

Price includes three sections with panels covered on one side with marokene leather fastened with metaline tacks.

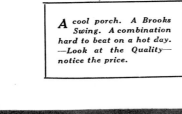

A cool porch. A Brooks Swing. A combination hard to beat on a hot day. —Look at the Quality— notice the price.

No. 404

No. 402

No. 404—Porch Swing

Brooks Price,
Plain Oak, $6.00

Dealers Price, $13.00

Height, 22 inches. Depth, 22 inches. **Length,** 60 inches. Shipping weight, 110 lbs.

Price includes galvanized chain and hammock hooks. Marokene leather covered cushion, $4.00 extra.

We allow for swings being 9 feet from ceiling. Additional length provided at 10 cents per ft.

No. 402—Porch Swing

Brooks Price,
Plain Oak, $9.50

Dealers Price, $20.00

Height, 24 inches. Depth, 22 inches. **Length,** 78 inches. Shipping weight, 170 lbs.

Price includes galvanized chain and hammock hooks. Marokene leather covered cushion, $5.00 extra.

You Save
From 25 Per Cent
to 50 Per Cent

WITH the issue of this catalog we list, in addition to our new designs in furniture, several lines of house furnishings of known and recognized quality and merit.

This innovation has been introduced at the request of our many customers and in the belief that our exceptional purchasing facilities would permit us to market standard goods at factory prices. It is our intention to add to these lines as the demand justifies, and the same care and attention will be exercised in selecting additional designs as has been given to those listed in the preceding pages.

By fortunate affiliations with other factories, we can now offer the consumer direct, exceptional values at prices that at first sight appear ridiculously low, but are occasioned by the elimination of middle profits and expenses, as a result of our modern selling plan.

Furnishings listed in this Section are
F. O. B., as follows:

Lace Curtains	Ann Arbor, Mich.
Rugs	Philadelphia, Pa.
Springs	Kenosha, Wis.
Kitchen Cabinet	Goshen, Ind.
Lamps	Bluffton, Ind.
Fiber Furniture	Jackson, Mich.
All other furnishings	Saginaw, Mich.

Fiber Furniture

THIS type of furniture meets with the growing demand for strong, sanitary and serviceable furniture appropriate for the den, library, living room, veranda, summerhouse, lawn or club house.

In addition to the adaptability of this furniture for general purposes it has the desirable feature of harmonizing with the various types of furniture now in general use, a single piece lending a tone of added luxury to any furnished room.

Since the advent of Arts and Crafts furniture with its ever growing popularity, appealing to those appreciative of quiet elegance and refinement, fiber furniture has been in greater demand for the reason that the quiet tones, the modest yet graceful lines, the comfortable proportions particularly blend with the Arts and Crafts.

Our fiber furniture is made of a tough, tenacious fiber subjected to a process of treatment that increases the strength of the fiber giving it wearing qualities that make it practically indestructible. It is then converted into strands of great strength and tenacity, and woven by hand into the dainty and comfort insuring designs shown. Fiber furniture is not affected by heat or moisture and has a finish that will not scratch, splinter or show the effects of hard usage or time. You can wash it if it is dusty, or scrub it if it's dirty—you can't hurt it.

Finish

Fiber furniture can be stained a variety of colors, but from experience, a rich toned brown or green will harmonize best with all our mission stains, and for that reason we encourage the selection of either of these two shades as we have been able to select tones of these colors, that have given general satisfaction.

It is imperative, to avoid delay, that you specify in your order whether you wish the green or brown finish.

Prices

All prices are F. O. B. Jackson, Mich. All fiber furniture will be shipped completely set up and, consequently, will take a higher freight rate than our knock down furniture, but the difference in weight will about equalize the total charge.

No. 705½F

No. 705½F—Rocker

Brooks Price, $9.50

Height, 33½ inches
Width, 26½ inches
Shipping Weight, 25 lbs.

No. 705F—Chair

Brooks Price, $9.00

Height, 33½ inches
Width, 26½ inches
Shipping Weight, 25 lbs.

No. 705F

No. 705SF

No. 705SF—Settee

Brooks Price, $14.50

Height, 33½ inches
Width, 44 inches
Shipping Weight, 35 lbs.

No. 726½F—Rocker

Brooks Price, $12.00

Height, 43 inches
Width, 32 inches
Shipping Weight, 35 lbs.

No. 726½F

No. 739F—Chair.   Brooks Price, $8.00
"   739½F—Rocker.   "   "   8.50

Height, 36 inches
Width, 34 inches
Shipping Weight, 20 lbs.

No. 739½F

No. 684F—Chair.   Brooks Price, $6.50
"   684½F—Rocker.   "   "   7.00

Height, 39 inches
Width, 31 inches
Shipping Weight, 25 lbs.

No. 684½F

No. 621½F—Rocker

Brooks Price, $3.75

Height, 37 inches
Width, 26½ inches
Shipping Weight, 18 lbs.

No. 621½F

No. 858F

No. 797F

Note that the writing shelf is hinged, which on being raised affords ample space for writing materials, etc. The No. 797 can be used to advantage in connection with No. 858 and is also a suitable chair for the reception hall, den or library.

No. 858F—Writing Desk

Brooks Price, $12.75

Height, 36 inches
Depth, 20 inches
Length, 34 inches
Shipping Weight, 40 lbs.
Quarter-sawed Oak Top.

No. 797F—Chair

Brooks Price, $4.00

Height, 38 inches
Width, 14 inches
Shipping Weight, 12 lbs.

No. 805KF

No. 804KF

No. 805KF—Center Table

Brooks Price, $5.75

Height, 28½ inches
Top, 24x26 inches
Shipping Weight, 25 lbs.

No. 804KF—Center Table

Brooks Price, $5.75

Height, 30 inches
Top, 27 inches in diameter
Shipping Weight, 25 lbs.

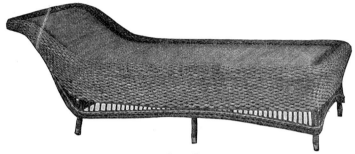
No. 862F

No. 862F—Couch

Brooks Price, $18.75

Height, 26 inches.   Width, 33 inches.   Length, 74 inches.
Shipping Weight, 50 lbs.

No. 892F–Work Basket

Brooks Price, $5.00

Height, 30 inches
Depth, 11 inches
Width, 18 inches
Shipping Weight, 15 lbs.

This basket can also be used for a fern stand.

No. 605¾F—Sewing Rocker

Brooks Price, $2.75

Height, 35 inches
Width, 19 inches
Shipping Weight, 11 lbs.

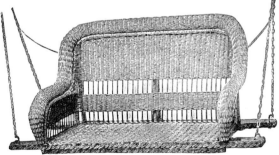

No. 892F

No. 605¾F

No 409F

No. 409F—Porch Swing

Brooks Price (Length 54 inches), $12.75
"   "   ("   66   "   ), $14.75
"   "   ("   78   "   ), $16.75

Prices include Hammock Hooks and 9 feet of Chain. Additional Chain at 8 cents per foot.
Shipping Weights: 54 inches, 40 lbs.; 66 inches, 50 lbs.; 78 inches, 60 lbs.

Arts and Crafts Lighting Fixtures

HOW often one feels an unconscious lack of finish, a coldness, to what at first sight conveys the impression of being a beautifully and artistically appointed room. The furniture, rugs, curtains, pictures, wall and ceiling decorations blend harmoniously—produce an effect that is pleasing to the eye and also giving evidence of discriminating taste. Still there is something that interferes with the air of completeness, and you then realize the inconsistency of the glaring brass or metal lighting fixtures. Fortunately, however, modern methods and ideas have had a decided tendency to supplant these inartistic yet essential fixtures by the use of materials that quietly conform to the general furnishings of the room. Highly polished metal is being superseded by wood, finished to conform to the general tones of the room. Clouded crystal in varying tints takes the place of the conventional frosted or grooved shades. With this end in view, we show in the pages following a line of portable lamps, domes and wall brackets, particularly appropriate when used in connection with our Arts and Crafts furniture.

Material

Solid oak alone is used in the wood work of these fixtures and every care and attention is given to insure perfect workmanship. Clouded opalescent glass, in tints that harmonize with Arts and Crafts designs, is used exclusively.

Equipment

All fixtures, whether electric, gas or oil are complete and ready for installation (except that we do not furnish electric bulbs). Such parts as electric sockets, wiring plugs, etc., gas hose, goose neck, mantel, burner, chimney, oil fount, wick, etc., are furnished with the different types of fixtures without extra charge. Insulating joints are included with combination fixtures.

Measurements

The length of a fixture means the distance between extreme points. We are prepared to furnish extra length of wood chain at 5c per link. The prices quoted are for the fixtures finished. in Dark weathered, Light weathered, Green weathered, Fumed, English or Flemish oak stain as desired.

Be sure and mention finish and color of glass and color of beads. You may have your choice in glass of green, green and brown or amber.

Unless your order specified these items, dark weathered finish will be sent and our judgment will be used as to the color of glass.

No. 392L

NO. 392L—Portable
Brooks Price, $8.50
Price includes leaded green art glass
and 4 inch seed fringe.
Height, 24 inches
Shade, 21 inches
Base, 8 x 8 inches
Equipped for 2 light electric
or one light gas.
Shipping Weight, 35 lbs.

Be sure and
specify electric or
gas equipment, also
your choice of the
finish desired, Dark
Weathered, Light
Weathered, Green
Weathered, Fumed,
English or Flemish
Oak.

No. 447L

NO. 447L—Portable
Brooks Price, $13.00
Price includes plain art glass. With
4 inch seed beads $1.25 extra.
This portable has pull sockets.
Height, 26 inches
Shade, 18 inches
Base, 7¼ inches square
Equipped for two light electric
or one light gas.
Shipping Weight, 30 lbs.

No. 63L

No. 63L—Portable
Brooks Price, $9.00
Price includes plain
art glass.
Height, 24 inches
Shade, 17½x17½ inches
Base, 10x10 inches
Shipping Weight, 25 lbs.
Equipped for two light
electric or one light gas.

No. 411L

No. 411L—Dome Lamp
Brooks Price, $8.50

No. 416L—Portable
Brooks Price, $6.50
Price includes plain art
glass.
Height, 23 inches
Shade, 14½x14½ inches
Base, 8 inches square
Shipping Weight, 25 lbs.
Equipped for two light
electric or one light gas.

No. 416L

Length, 54 inches. Spread, 20x20 inches. Depth of Apron, 4 inches. Electric or gas dome. Gas burner or
electric bulbs not furnished. Made only in leaded green art glass. Shipping Weight, 50 lbs.

No. 174L

You may have your choice of green, green and brown or amber art glass. Be sure to specify the color wanted, also electric or gas equipment.

No. 311L

No. 174L—Portable
Brooks Price, $7.00

Equipped for 2 lights, electric.
Height, 24 inches
Shade, 14½ x 14½ inches
Base, 7 x 7 inches
Shipping Weight, 25 lbs.

No. 311L—Portable
Brooks Price, $4.00

Furnished either as a one light oil, gas or electric, as required.
Height, 24 inches
Shade, 14x14 inches
Base, 7x7 inches
Shipping Weight, 25 lbs.

No 400L

No. 410L

No. 354L

No. 400L—Portable
Brooks Price, $5.00

Furnished as a one light oil burner only.
Height, 20 inches
Shade, 11x11 inches
Base, 7x7 inches
Shipping Weight, 25 lbs.

No. 354L—Portable
Brooks Price, $3.25

Furnished either as a one light oil, gas or electric as required.
Height, 22 inches
Shade, 14½x14½ inches
Base, 7x7 inches
Shipping Weight, 25 lbs.

No. 410L—Dome
Brooks Price, $7.50

Length, 54 inches.   Dome, 20x20 inches.   Apron Depth, 4 inches.
Two light electric. Made only in green leaded art glass and woodwork stained in weathered oak.
Shipping Weight, 50 lbs.

No. 476L—Wall Bracket

Brooks Price, $5.50

Equipped for one light, electric. Plain art glass.

Extends from wall 12 inches

Drop, 17 inches

Lantern, 5x5x8 inches

Shipping Weight, 20 lbs.

No. 476L

No. 376L

No. 376L—Cluster

Five-light, electric, Ceiling Fixture.

Brooks Price, $16.00

Price quoted is for plain art glass only; for leaded art glass as shown, $4.00 extra.

Length, 24 inches
Ceiling Plate, 18x18 inches
Small Shades, 7x7 inches
Shipping Weight, 60 lbs.

No. 474L—Dome
Brooks Price, $10.50

Price quoted is without beads. With four-inch seed beads, $1.50 extra. Dome is equipped for one or four electric lights. Furnished in leaded art glass only.

Length, 60 inches
Spread, 21 inches
Ceiling Plate, 8 inches
Shipping Weight, 30 lbs.

No. 474L

No. 93L

No. 93L—Wall Bracket

Brooks Price, $5.50

Equipped for one light, electric. Price includes leaded art glass panels, as shown.

Extends from wall 10 inches
Drop, 15 inches
Lantern, 4½x4½x7 inches.
Shipping Weight, 15 lbs.

The very best values in framed mirrors on the market today.

No. 214M

Brooks Price, { Bevel Mirror, $3.50
{ Plain Mirror, $3.00

A popular pattern of excellent design. Frame is two inches wide, finished in white enamel. Will not chip or change color. The ideal mirror for the bath room. Fitted with a 16x20 inch French mirror.

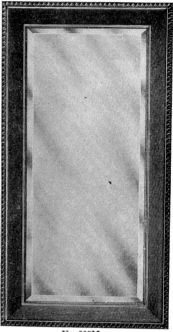

No. 207M

Brooks Price, { Bevel Mirror, $6.50
{ Plain Mirror, $6.00

Absolutely the best value in a mirror ever offered. Frame is 4 inches wide and made of solid oak. Colonial moulding on outer edges. Finished in a rich brown Mission. Fitted with an 18x40 inch French mirror.

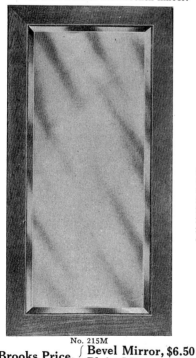

From the standpoint of style, high class workmanship and finish these mirrors cannot be excelled.

No. 215M

Brooks Price, { Bevel Mirror, $6.50
{ Plain Mirror, $6.00

A nobby design of severe yet dignified lines. Frame is 4 inches wide and made of solid oak. Furnished in Golden oak or Early English finish as desired. Fitted with an 18x40 inch French mirror.

No. 212M

Brooks Price, { Bevel Mirror, $4.00
{ Plain Mirror, $3.50

A new design of increasing popularity. Frame is 3½ inches wide, finished in smooth, mat gilt, and mounted with center ornaments, burnished in gold. Fitted with a 16x20 inch French mirror.

No. 1 C and No. 2 C

Eight-Day Mission Clocks

Height, 19½ inches
Width, 12¾ inches

The cases are made of specially prepared wood and have a smooth Flemish, Mission Oak finish, with gun metal door hinges and latch. Fitted with Eight-Day movements, hour and half-hour strike on rich Cathedral gong. 5½ inch dial with polished gilt hands and dial numerals. Visible pendulum with polished brass ball.

No 1 C

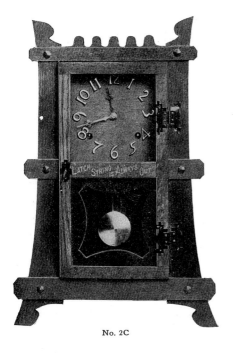

No. 2C

Brooks Price

No. 1 C $4.00
No. 2 C 4.00

These clocks are remarkable values, excellent time keepers and are appropriate for the den, hall, library or living room.

No. 618BK

No. 618BK—Kitchen Cabinet

Brooks Price, $19.50

Height, 68 inches
Width, 37 inches
Depth, Base, 25 inches

This Cabinet has sliding top; the front and ends are of solid oak, finished Golden Oak Waxed. Has a self feeding sifter flour bin in top, with full glass front; will hold 50 lbs. of flour. The sifter can be removed. The China Cupboard in top is fitted with one shelf. The three top doors are glazed with Queen Anne glass. Just below the China Cupboard is a tilting sugar bin. Just below the bin are two small racks for the rolling pin, and metal scoop for the sugar, both of which are furnished. The lower part of the top has two panel doors which carry a card rack for receipts, bread and milk checks, etc., and spice, tea and coffee jars. We furnish free of charge five glass spice jars, one tea jar and one coffee jar, attached to the doors with metal racks. The screw caps are of aluminum. The top of base can be pulled forward, giving a working space of 40x37 inches. This entire extension top is covered with nickeled zinc. Just below the extension top we have a sliding cutting board of clear white wood, both sides nicely sanded. The top drawer is for small kitchen utensils, the second drawer is the linen drawer, and the bottom drawer contains a two compartment metal Bread and Cake Box, with hinged cover for each compartment. This Bread Box can be removed, as can also the tilting bin and drawers. The large Cupboard in the base is fitted with sliding tray shelf. The large door to the Cupboard part carries a neat pan rack and is fitted with a special push-button pull.

Shipping Weight, 208 lbs.

No. 6K–Kitchen Table Cabinet

Brooks Price, $4.25

Height, 30 inches
Top, 26x42 inches
Shipping Weight, 65 lbs.

No. 6K

Do not compare No. 6 Cabinet with cheap imitations. The top is of clean white basswood, and the frame is of select softwood, finished in imitation golden oak. The legs are turned hardwood. The right hand sliding bin will hold 40 lbs. of flour, while the left hand bin is divided for meal, sugar, etc. These bins have metal bottoms. The large cutlery drawer and the sliding carving and kneading board add to the convenience of this Cabinet. Trimmings are of antique copper.

No. 4226K—Kitchen Cabinet

Brooks Price, $13.50

Height, 70 inches

Top, 42 x 26 inches

The entire front of this Cabinet is made of oak, the same kind of high grade material as we use in the construction of our other Cabinets. The Cabinet is finished Golden Oak wax and trimmed with copper hardware. You will note the ends and back extend two inches above the top, giving the Cabinet a very neat and finished appearance, in addition to providing a very useful top shelf. The roomy China Compartment has two wide shelves and tight fitting glass doors. Just below the China Closet are two drawers for small articles, two tilting bins, one for sugar and one for salt and a shelf for spice jars. The top of the base is made of clear whitewood 26x42 inches. The base contains a handy cutlery drawer, sliding cutlery board, and a large, comodious tilting flour bin which will hold fifty pounds of flour. The compartment for kettles, pans, etc., is equipped with a sliding tray-shelf and pan rack on the door. The interior of the top and the inside of the doors are varnished. Casters furnished.

Shipping weight, 175 pounds.

No. 0018K

Fireless Cookers

Our Fireless Cookers are made with hardwood frames and iron panels, finished in beautiful standard colors. Covers lay straight back and rest on folding brackets capable of sustaining 500 pounds. Linings and utensils are of pure aluminum, rust proof and sanitary Easiest in the world to keep clean. They are based on scientific, sanitary and hygienic principles, the result of long study, extensive and exhaustive experiment, and persistent effort to obtain perfect stoves.

YOU WANT A FIRELESS COOKER, BECAUSE

1. It cooks anything which can be cooked on a gas or kitchen range, and in the same length of time.
2. The food will be cooked better, taste better and be more digestible than if cooked in any other way.
3. It soon saves enough gas, coal or wood to pay for itself.
4. It makes cooking day easy for the housewife or servant. After starting food cooking and closing covers, it requires no further attention until you wish to use it, as it will not over-cook, boil dry or burn. Ready to serve at your convenience.

No. 1—One Compartment

No. 2—Two Compartments

5. The toughest meat is made tender. When roasting, no basting is necessary.
6. Our Cookers retain cold as well as heat and preserve ices in one compartment while food is cooking in the other.
7. Breakfast may be placed in the Cooker in the evening, dinner in the cool of the morning.

Brooks Price, With gas and electric burners, $14 Without burners, $10

EQUIPMENT

One 8-quart pure aluminum kettle with self-locking cover. One pair tongs. One wire rack. Self-stopping hinges and folding brackets. Pure aluminum linings throughout. Complete gas equipment. One gas burner in bottom of well for boiling, stewing, baking and roasting. One burner on cover for use in browning when baking or roasting. Also can be used for frying or anything which can be done on a gas or kitchen range.

Brooks Price, With gas and electric burners, $24 Without burners, $16

EQUIPMENT

One 8-quart and one 4-quart pure aluminum kettles with self-locking covers. One pair tongs. Two wire racks. Self-stopping hinges and folding brackets. Pure aluminum linings throughout. Complete gas equipment. One burner in each well for boiling, stewing, baking and roasting. Burner on each cover for browning when baking or roasting. Cover burners can be used for frying or anything which can be done on a gas or kitchen range.

When gas or electricity is not available the disks may be heated on any stove. Full directions with each cooker as to roasting, baking, stewing and boiling with and without burners.

With each Cooker is furnished a cook-book giving full instructions as to the operation of the cooker as well as valuable recipes, useful to every housekeeper.

No. 3—Three Compartments

Brooks Price, With gas and electric burners, $31. Without burners, $19

EQUIPMENT

One 8-quart and two 4-quart pure aluminum kettles with self-locking covers. One pair tongs. Three wire racks. Self-stopping hinges and folding brackets. Pure aluminum linings throughout. Complete gas equipment. One burner in each well for boiling, stewing, baking and roasting. Burner on each cover for browning when baking or roasting. Cover burners can be used for frying or anything which can be done on a gas or kitchen range.

Lace Curtains

To meet the constant demand for quality goods at reasonable prices, we feel that in presenting the following illustrations and prices of lace curtains, another step has been taken toward bringing the consumer in closer contact with the producer, dispensing entirely with the necessity on the part of the former of paying ridiculous prices in order to cover all the profits and expenses of the retailer or middleman.

After a thorough investigation, as to the material and designs in popular favor, we have decided to list the celebrated Nottingham weave, together with cotton laces mounted on light nets, which are excellent imitations of the real lace, and also real Cluny lace curtains mounted on the best quality of French nets.

The popularity of the Nottingham weave is well recognized. The designs, well woven on serviceable net, are the result of years of careful study of popular demand. For serviceability and durability, considering price, they are exceptional bargains—bargains that will be immediately recognized by the shrewd buyer.

The real Cluny lace curtains cannot be excelled in quality or value. Real Cluny lace is imported, and is made by hand by the peasants of the villages in the interior of France. It will be easy, for even the casual observer, to note the superiority of these goods from the illustrations only. The lace is made from real linen and mounted on the finest of French net. The corners instead of being turned by machine, as in the ordinary curtain, become a part of the design.

The Cotton laces are machine made, imported from England, and mounted on French nets. They are exceptionally good imitations of the real lace curtains, and are remarkable values for the prices listed.

Dimensions

Are given under each illustration and apply to **each curtain of the pair.** For example, 2½ yds., by 45 inches means that each curtain of the pair is 2½ yds. by 45 inches wide.

Prices

All prices are quoted by the pair, and the price is the same for either the white or ecru (tan). Be sure and state the color wanted when ordering, or white net will invariably be sent to you.

Shipping

Express rates are practically the same as mailing rates, but where two or more pairs are ordered it is usually best to ship via Express, as delivery is safer and we **advise** this means of shipment.

Samples

We cannot send samples of the laces, but all curtains are sold subject to approval of the purchaser and may be returned at our expense if not satisfactory.

No. 35569 C

Brooks Price, $1.00 Per Pair

3 yards by 52 inches
In White only
Nottingham Weave

No. 35450 C

Brooks Price, $1.25 Per Pair

3 yards by 54 inches
In White only
Nottingham Weave

No. 35710 C

Brooks Price, $1.50 Per Pair

3 yards by 54 inches
In White or Arabian
Nottingham Weave

No. 35868 W C

Brooks Price, $1.50 Per Pair

3 yards by 51 inches
In White, Arabian or Ivory
Nottingham Weave

No. 35896 C
Brooks Price, $1.90 Per Pair

3 yards by 51 inches
In White only
Nottingham Weave

No. 35638 C
Brooks Price, $2.25 Per Pair

3 yards by 53 inches
In White only
Nottingham Weave

No. 35501 W C
Brooks Price, $2.35 Per Pair

3 yards by 51 inches
In White only
Nottingham Weave

No. 35252 W C
Brooks Price, $2.35 Per Pair

3 yards by 51 inches
In White only
Nottingham Weave

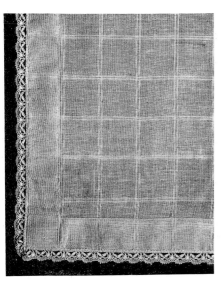

No. 461 C
Brooks Price, $2.00 Per Pair

2½ yards by 38 inches
In White or Ecru
Cotton Lace or Plaid Scrim

No. 8092 C
Brooks Price, $1.75 Per Pair

2½ yards by 40 inches
In White or Ecru
Cotton, Imitation Cluny

No. 8108 C
Brooks Price, $2.50 Per Pair

2½ yards by 40 inches
In White or Ecru
Cotton, Imitation Cluny

No. 8110 C
Brooks Price, $2.75 Per Pair

2½ yards by 40 inches
In White or Ecru
Cotton, Imitation Cluny

No. 8098 C

Brooks Price, $2.50 Per Pair

2½ yards by 40 inches
In White or Ecru
Cotton, Imitation Cluny

No. 453 C

Brooks Price, $2.50 Per Pair

2½ yards by 40 inches
In White or Ecru
Imitation Cluny Lace mounted on
Plaid Scrim

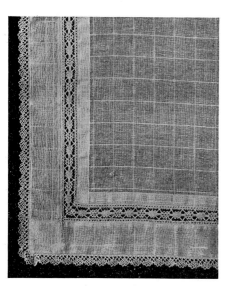

No. 457 C

Brooks Price, $2.75 Per Pair

2½ yards by 38 inches
In White or Ecru
Imitation Cluny Lace in Cotton mounted
on Plaid Scrim

No. 455 C

Brooks Price, $3.25 Per Pair

2½ yards by 40 inches
In White or Ecru
Imitation Cluny Lace in Cotton on
Plaid Scrim

No. 2048 C
Brooks Price, $2.50 Per Pair

2½ yards by 45 inches
In White or Ecru
Real Cluny Lace, Pure Linen on Fine
French Net

No. 2104 C
Brooks Price, $5.00 Per Pair

2½ yards by 45 inches
In White or Ecru
Real Cluny Lace, Pure Linen on Fine
French Net

No. 2332 C
Brooks Price, $6.00 Per Pair

2½ yards by 45 inches
In White or Ecru
Real Cluny Lace, Pure Linen on Fine
French Net

No. 2178 C
Brooks Price, $7.00 Per Pair

2½ yards by 45 inches
In White or Ecru
Real Cluny Lace, Pure Linen on Fine
French Net

Rugs

A S a result of the insistent demand on the part of our customers for Oriental rugs that will blend harmoniously with modern interior decorations, rugs that will be particularly appropriate in carrying out the restful and artistic color schemes of the well appointed room, we list the patterns shown on the following pages. We aim to show all that is best in Oriental art and weaving, reproduced by modern methods of manufacture. The materials used are equivalent in quality and texture to those used by Oriental weavers, but woven with greater skill and care as well as by improved, and consequently more sanitary methods, resulting in a far more desirable, wear-proof fabric than could ever be produced by crude hand methods.

We aim to place on the market a product as fine in texture as those made by the hand weavers of the Orient, with guaranteed wearing qualities and at about one tenth the price. The designs selected have the unqualified endorsement of the best decorators.

Experience has demonstrated that it is impossible to thoroughly illustrate, even by colored plates, the true beauty and harmony of color of any rug of Oriental design. It must be seen in order that its true value will be appreciated. It is on this account, that we make no effort at display in colored illustrations endeavoring only to show the general design. The color description under each rug gives a fairly adequate idea of the general effect as well as of the predominating color, which will be of service in ordering so as to carry out any color scheme that may be contemplated.

In addition to this, our rugs are backed by our guarantee, which means that if they are not entirely satisfactory they can be returned and your money refunded. You take no risk. Our confidence in our selection, from every source of supply, justifies us in assuming entire responsibility on this point. We know you will be satisfied and that any selection you make, providing the pattern and general tone, as specified under each illustration, is satisfactory to you, will more than exceed your expectations. You are to be the sole judge.

The following list gives the prices as well as the various sizes in which the different patterns are manufactured:

Auburn Body Brussels Rugs

Size	Price	2242 1R	2197 R	2234 2R	2240 1R
4ft. 6in. x 7ft. 6in.	$7.20	X	—	X	—
6ft. x 9ft.	13.40	X	—	X	—
9ft. x 9ft.	17.85	X	—	X	X
8ft. 3in. x 10ft. 6in.	20.00	X	X	X	X
9ft. x 10ft. 6in.	20.85	X	—	X	X
9ft. x 12ft.	22.00	X	X	X	X
9ft. x 15ft.	29.85	X	—	X	X
10ft. 6in. x 12ft.	29.85	X	—	X	—
10ft. 6in. x 13ft. 6in.	33.60	X	—	X	—
11ft. 3in x 12ft.	29.85	X	—	X	—
11ft. 3in. x 15ft.	37.35	X	—	X	—

X Indicates size that rug can be furnished in.

Tanjore Wilton Rugs

Size	Price	410 R	390 R	281 R	471 R
1ft. 10in. x 3ft.	$2.15	X	X	X	—
2ft. 3in. x 4ft. 6in.	3.20	X	X	X	X
3ft. x 5ft. 3in.	5.35	X	—	X	X
6ft. 9in. x 9ft.	21.35	—	X	—	X
6ft. 9in. x 12ft.	26.15	—	X	—	X
8ft. 3in. x 10ft. 6in.	28.25	X	X	X	X
9ft. x 12ft.	30.95	X	X	X	X
10ft. 6in. x 12ft.	42.65	—	—	X	X
11ft. 3in. x 12ft.	42.65	—	X	—	X
10ft. 6in. x 13ft. 6in.	48.00	—	—	X	X
11ft. 3in. x 13ft.6in.	50.00	—	X	—	X
11ft. 3in. x 15ft.	53.35	—	X	—	X

— Indicates that rug is not made in that size.

Auburn Body Brussels Rugs

No. 2240—1 R

Color—Combination of red, brown, green and tan. Brown and red predominating.

No. 2234—2 R

Color—Combination of green, brown, buff and tan. An olive green predominating.

See page 56 for prices.

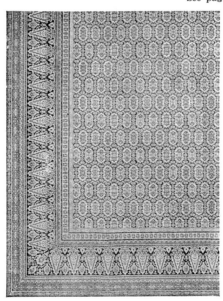

No. 2242—1R

Color—Combination of brown, green and terra cotta with brown predominating. Also made with green as strongest color.

No. 2197—R

Color—Combination of brown, buff, red, terra cotta, green and black. Rich brown predominating.

Tanjore Wilton Rugs

No. 390 R

Color—Combination of deep red, terra cotta and black, with red predominating.

No. 281 R

Color—Combination of green, brown, buff and black, with green predominating.

See page 56 for prices

No. 410 R

Color—Combination of brown, green, tan and red, with green and brown predominating.

No. 471 R

Color—Combination of red, black, brown and tan, with red and black predominating.

Asbestos Table Covers

Our Folding Asbestos Table Covers with detachable flannel covers offer perfect protection to finished surfaces from the decidedly injurious effects of hot dishes. They are made from sheets of pure asbestos on both sides of a wool center, which provides the necessary elasticity, and are covered with detachable flannel jackets, which are easily removed and washed.

Both leaves and pads fold in convenient sections and are shipped in attractive boxes. Prices cover either round or square top tables.

Size of Table	Mat	Extra Leaves
42 inches	each, $3.50	each, $0.90
48 inches	each, 4.00	each, 1.00
54 inches	each, 4.50	each, 1.05

Table Linen

We are now able to list under our guarantee, of satisfaction or money refunded, "Pure Linen Irish Damask" Table linen, full bleached, in the various popular patterns of the day. They are remarkable values, fully 25 per cent lower in price than the price charged by your local dealer.

We can furnish the following patterns both for table cloths and napkins: Rose and Honeysuckle, Pansy Wreath and Ribbon, Poppies, Chrysanthemums, Daisy and Stripe, Fleur de Lis and Shamrock, Iris and Fleur de Lis, and the Chrysanthemum and Shamrock.

Prices

TABLE CLOTHS	NAPKINS
70 in. wide by 72 in. long ..$1.90	20 in. square, per doz $2.25
70 in. wide by 90 in. long .. 2.35	22 in. square, per doz...... 2.65
70 in. wide by 108 in. long .. 2.80	24 in. square, per doz....... 2.95

Prices quoted are for sufficient material only to make table cloth and napkins of size given. Napkins furnished in lots of one dozen only.

Be sure and specify pattern and size wanted.

Sundries

Stain, any color listed	per half-pint, $0.25
Stain, any color listed	per pint, .40
Prepared Furniture Wax	per ¼-lb., .15
Prepared Furniture Wax	per ½-lb., .25
Stain Brushes	each, .10
Marokene Leather, any color listed	per square foot, .20
Genuine Leather	per square foot, .40

Unless otherwise specified, all orders for sundries, excepting stains, will be sent by mail, postage rate 16 cents per pound. Stains must be sent by express, as the law prohibits mailing same. In your remittance kindly include sufficient money to cover postage.

The E-Z Suction Cleaner

(Patents Applied For)

Lightest. Easiest. Sucks Most Dust, Requires Least Effort. E-Z for Mamma's Helper

Brooks Price, $7.50

"Truth is stranger than fiction"

Read and be convinced

IT is with extreme satisfaction we announce the completion of negotiations for the privilege of offering our trade an exceptional opportunity to obtain, at a ridiculously low price, the very latest creation in Vacuum Cleaners, known as the E-Z Suction Cleaner and for which patents are pending.

The machine is hand operated and weighs but four pounds. Is exceptionally easy to operate, as shown in the illustration, which is an actual reproduction of the machine in use in our city. The large 7⅛-inch bellows, 25 inches long, sucks over 800 inches of air (the fundamental principal of vacuum cleaning) and cleans thoroughly a strip 8 inches wide at each stroke, which is a greater efficiency than that possessed by many of the larger machines costing three times the price and requiring five times the amout of labor.

The construction is extremely simple, there being no complicated parts to get out of order, no crooked passages to retard the air, no friction in bellows, valves, pipe or screen, no metal cylinders to become easily damaged and difficult to operate, no permanent screen to clog with dust.

The material is of the very best quality throughout. The bellows cloth is superbly flexible and long lived. The valves are of water-proof wood fiber, extremely light and quick acting. The screens are simply of muslin, easily dusted or washed.

Every bit of the operator's effort goes into productive dust-lifting work; not in needless friction in pipes and parts of the cleaner.

THE E-Z SUCTION CLEANER gets the dust that is everywhere, the grit and dirt deep in the carpet and everything not too large to pass into the nozzle. The grit cuts out the carpet by sawing into the fibre at every step. The saving in carpet alone will pay for the E-Z CLEANER many times every year. The loose dirt and paper pieces, so hard to get with broom and sweeper from the corners and cracks, enter the E-Z CLEANER like magic and the room quickly looks neat and tidy. No dusting necessary. Ten to twenty minutes will clean a large room and take out a surprising amount of dirt, eliminating an unsanitary condition which may cause consumption, typhoid and various nose, throat and lung diseases.

You cannot afford to be without one of these E-Z SUCTION CLEANERS. It means health and happiness to your home at very little expense.

This machine has been on the market but a few weeks and already the demand is enormous. We advise ordering early to insure prompt delivery.

Many of the very best homes in the cities of Grand Rapids, Bay City, Detroit and Saginaw are equipped with the E-Z SUCTION CLEANER, and numerous testimonials vouching for the exceptional merits of this machine have been received, but owing to the limited space we can offer but the following

Gentlemen:

Saginaw, Mich.

It was my privilege to purchase the first suction cleaner offered for sale by the E-Z Suction Cleaner Company of this city. I am pleased to say that the cleaner has proved a most valuable addition to the furnishings of our household. It is exactly what the name suggests—an effective cleaner, and it is easy to operate, and at the low retail price should find a place in every home.

Yours truly, JOSEPH P. TRACY
Secretary, Saginaw Boad of Trade.

Gentlemen :

Saginaw, Michigan, December 9, 1911

The E-Z Suction Cleaner is an article of great value to a busy house-keeper.

Having used the electrical vacuum cleaner, I find this much more simple. The work is accomplished as easily as with an ordinary carpet sweeper when directions given are carried out.

Respectfully yours, MARY S. SYMONS

Bed Springs—Standard Sizes

The special feature of our springs are the rigid base and unusual strength coupled with extreme lightness of weight.

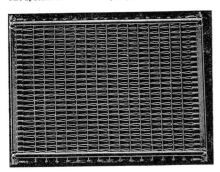

No. 151—Tubulars

1½-inch Tubing, 2 inches by 1½ inches by 5-32 inch angle ends. Fifty-four No. 12 wire helicals, and four No. 11 wire helicals. ⅝ inch No. 16 band iron sides, aluminum finish. Bronze frame. Malleable castings, 6 inch raise. Equipped with double rod linkless fabric, which will never become unfastened or sag and is absolutely noiseless and smooth.

Shipping Weight 65 lbs.

Brooks Price, $3.30

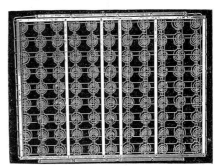

No. 1—Model

Ninety-nine No. 11½ Premier Springs, 6 inches high No. 6½ Border. Six 1 inch by 1 inch by ⅛ inch Angle slats. Twenty No. 11½ cross rods. Bottom angle frame being reinforced with wire rods that are fastened onto wire border that is held in place by laying between angle iron sides. This construction insures absolutely no sagging of the springs and that the angle iron slats will always stay rigid.

Shipping Weight, 65 lbs.

Brooks Price, $3.35

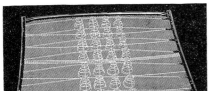

No. 500—Tubes

1¼-inch Tube sides bent, 1½-inch raise 1½-inches by 1½ inches by 3-16 inch angle ends, with 2 inches by ⅛ inch baton strips.
Single Pencil weave fabric and seven ribs of five wires each. No. 12 wires on edge, one on each edge.
Shipping Weight, 55 lbs., Plain
Shipping Weight, 65 lbs., Three Row

Brooks Price, 3 Row, $2.80; Plain, $2.25

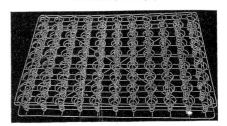

No. 100
Single Cone for Wood Bed

Ninety-nine coils, No. 11½ Premier wire, No. 6½ Border, 6½-inch springs.

Shipping Weight, 35 lbs.

Brooks Price, $1.75

Combination Davenport Bed

This is a strongly built all-iron combination folding Divan and Davenport and Bed. The frame used throughout is of angle iron which, together with the ends, is finished in Gold Bronze. The wire used in this Divan is of the best quality procurable, which will not sag. Oil Tempered Helicals and spirals insure comfort with durability.

Can be converted into a bed, cot, davenport, divan or cradle at a moment's notice. A useful piece of furniture for any home.

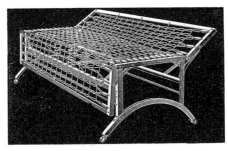

No. 129—Sanitary Couch
Brooks Price, $3.50

We have gone to considerable expense in inventing and perfecting the simple but practicable lock that goes to make up one of the main features of this cheap but well built article. Width of seat, 23 inches; height of seat, 17½ inches; wide open, 45 inches; length, 72 inches. Shipping weight, 70 pounds. This combination Divan and Davenport and Bed is bound to please the most exacting.

Ideal Furnishings ⒷⓂⒸ at Factory Prices

Freight Rates in Cents Per 100 Pounds

	A	B	C	D	E	F	G	H	I	J	K	Min. Frt. Charge
ALABAMA .... MOBILE	$0.95	$0.95	$0.95	$0.95	$1.16	$1.10		$1.10	$2.32	$1.23	$1 18	$1.16
ARIZONA...... PHOENIX, TEMPE, PRESCOTT	2.63	2.63	2.19	3.05	3.05	2.90		2.63	9.15	3.50	3.50	2.63
ARKANSAS.............. LITTLE ROCK	1.18	1.24	1.05	1.40	1.46	1.20		1.22	4.20	1.60	1.88	1.46
CALIFORNIA..... SAN FRANCISCO, SAN JOSE												
" ...LOS ANGELES, SACRAMENTO	1.75	2.60	2.20	3.00	3.00	3.00		2.60	9.00	2.60	2.60	2 60
COLORADO.............. DENVER, PUEBLO	1.61	1.67	1.40	2.02	2.08	2.05		1.63	6.24	2.03	2.50	1.47
CONNECTICUT............... ALL POINTS	.56	.66	.66	.66	.76	.82		.79	2.28	.25	.22	.82
DELAWARE................. ALL POINTS	.52	.60	.60	.60	.69	.75		.69	1.98	.23	.42	.75
DIST. OF COLUMBIA.......... ALL POINTS	.48	.57	.57	.57	.66	.72		.69	1.98	.33	.42	.72
FLORIDA.................... PENSACOLA	.95	.95	.95	.95	1.16	1.10		1.30	2.32	1.03	1.23	1.16
GEORGIA..................... SAVANNAH	1.11	1.17	1.17	1.17	1.38	1.30		1.35	3.17	.70	.87	1.38
IDAHO........ POCATELLO, COUER D'ALENE	2.62	2.68	2.30	3.15	3.21	2.85		2.71	9.63	3.50	3.60	2.37
ILLINOIS...................... CHICAGO	.27	.32	.32	.32	.37	.37		.25	.99	.65	.75	.37
"......................... CAIRO	.38	.45	.45	.45	.50	.47		.45	1.51	.78	.90	.51
INDIANA........ INDIANAPOLIS, RICHMOND	.29	.34	.34	.34	.40	.32		.32	1.11	.60	.70	.40
IOWA............ CLINTON, DAVENPORT	.57	.61	.55	.70	.74	.38		.52	1.65	.84	.97	.62
KANSAS.................. LEAVENWORTH	.78	.84	.75	1.00	1.06	.80		.81	3.18	1.39	1.39	.81
"....................... TOPEKA	1.03	1.09	.94	1.29	1.35	1.09		.81	4.05	1.68	1.68	1.00
KENTUCKY.................. LOUISVILLE	.33	.39	.39	.39	.45	.41		.41	1.29	.65	.75	.45
LOUISIANA.... NEW ORLEANS, BATON ROUGE	.95	.95	.95	.95	1.16	1.10		1.10	2.32	.98	1.18	1.16
MAINE...................... PORTLAND	.56	.66	.66	.66	.76	.82		.79	2.28	.34	.27	.82
MARYLAND................. ALL POINTS	.48	.57	.57	.57	.66	.72		.69	1.98	.38	.42	.72
MASSACHUSETTS............ ALL POINTS	.56	.66	.66	.66	.76	.82		.79	2.28	.34	.14	.82
MICHIGAN.................... DETROIT	.20	.24	.24	.24	.28	.37		.30	.59	.51	.59	.37
"................... GRAND RAPIDS	.22	.26	.26	.26	.30	.33		.25	.79	.62	.72	.33
MINNESOTA. DULUTH, ST. PAUL, MINNEAP'S	.56	.66	.66	.66	.78	.65		.78	2.34	.99	1.15	.78
MISSISSIPPI........ VICKSBURG, NATCHEZ	.95	.95	.95	.95	1.16	1.10		1.10	2.32	.98	1.18	1.16
MISSOURI................... ST. LOUIS	.34	.40	.40	.40	.46	.44		.43	1.38	.76	.88	.46
"........... KANSAS CITY, ST. JOSEPH	.78	.84	.75	1.00	1.06	.80		.81	3.18	1.53	1.39	.81
MONTANA..... BUTTE, HELENA, ANACONDA	2.46	2.56	2.24	2.91	3.03	2.85		2.68	9.09	4.36	3.40	2.36
NEBRASKA..................... OMAHA	.78	.84	.75	1.00	1.06	.80		.81	3.18	1.14	1.39	.81
NEVADA................ CARSON CITY	2.88	2.88	2.44	3.25	3.30	3.15		2.88	9.90	3.70	2.80	2.88
"........................ RENO	2.63	2.63	2.19	3.05	3.05	2.90		2.63	9.15	3.45	2.60	2.63
NEW HAMPSHIRE............. ALL POINTS	.56	.66	.66	.66	.76	.82		.79	2.28	.34	.24	.82
NEW JERSEY................ ALL POINTS	.56	.65	.65	.65	.74	.80		.72	2.07	.18	.35	.80
NEW MEXICO................. SANTA FE	2.24	2.30	2.10	2.52	2.58	2.32		2.33	7.74	2.66	3.00	2.16
"....................... DEMING	2.07	2.07	1.86	2.40	2.40	2.25		2.07	7.20	2.85	2.85	2.07
NEW YORK............ NEW YORK CITY	.51	.60	.60	.60	.69	.75		.72	2.07	.09	.18	.75
"...................... BUFFALO	.32	.38	.38	.38	.44	.45		.43	1.29	.33	.43	.45
"..................... SYRACUSE	.41	.48	.48	.48	.55	.72		.57	1.65	.30	.38	.72
NORTH CAROLINA.......... WILMINGTON	.89	.97	.97	.97	1.16	1.17		1.17	3.48	.79	.83	1.17
NORTH DAKOTA.................. FARGO	1.01	1.11	1.02	1.20	1.32	1.14		1.52	3.96	1.85	1.82	1.23
OHIO......................... TOLEDO	.20	.24	.24	.24	.28	.37		.30	.57	.51	.59	.37
"..................... CINCINNATI	.31	.37	.37	.37	.43	.40		.40	1.15	.57	.65	.40
OKLAHOMA..... OKLAHOMA CITY, EL RENO	1.42	1.49	1.37	1.70	1.76	1.50		1.36	5.10	1.96	2.18	1.43
OREGON........... PORTLAND, ASTORIA	1.75	2.60	2.20	3.00	3.00	3.00		2.60	9.00	2 60	2.60	2.60
PENNSYLVANIA.......... PHILADELPHIA	.48	.59	.59	.59	.67	.73		.70	2.01	.30	.35	.73
"..................... PITTSBURG	.32	.38	.38	.38	.44	.45		.45	1.29	.39	.50	.45
RHODE ISLAND.............. ALL POINTS	.56	.66	.66	.66	.76	.82		.79	2.28	.30	.19	.82
SOUTH CAROLINA.......... CHARLESTON	1.03	1.12	1.12	1.12	1.31	1.30		1.35	3.25	.70	.87	1.31
SOUTH DAKOTA...... SIOUX FALLS, CANTON	.81	.87	.77	1.03	1.09	.83		.83	2.49	1.39	1.53	.83
TENNESSEE................... MEMPHIS	.70	.70	.70	.70	.91	.85		.85	2.73	1.00	1.00	.91
TEXAS.............. HOUSTON, GALVESTON	1.60	1.60	1.31	1.87	1.87	1.57		1.56	5.61	2.23	2.35	1.31
"............ AUSTIN, SAN ANTONIA	1.60	1.60	1.31	1.87	1.87	1.57		1.56	5.61	2.23	2.35	1.31
UTAH............ OGDEN, SALT LAKE CITY	2.23	2.29	2.03	2.67	2.73	2.45		2.60	9.33	3.41	3.53	2.34
VERMONT.................. ALL POINTS	.56	.66	.66	.66	.76	.82		.79	2.28	.43	.45	.82
VIRGINIA.... RICHM'D, NORFOLK, ROANOKE	.48	.57	.57	.57	.66	.72		.69	1.98	.32	1.20	.72
WASHINGTON............ SEATTLE, TACOMA	1.75	2.60	2.20	3.00	3.00	3.00		2.60	9.00	2.60	2.60	2.60
"........ VANCOUVER, ABERDEEN	1.75	2.60	2.20	3.00	3.00	3.00		2.60	9.00	2.60	2.60	2.60
WISCONSIN................. MILWAUKEE	.30	.35	.35	.35	.41	.25		.30	1.17	.65	.75	.41
"...................... MADISON	.52	.65	.65	.65	.77	.39		.42	2.28	.65	1.07	.77
WYOMING................... CHEYENNE	1.61	1.67	1.40	2.02	2.08	2.05		1.63	9.24	2.38	2.50	1.47
CANADA............ VANCOUVER, VICTORIA	1.80	2.65	2.25	3.05	3.05	3.05		2.60	9.15	2.65	2.65	2.65
"...................... WINNIPEG	1.31	1.41	1.41	1.55	1.67	1.72		1.67	5.01	1.88	2.04	1.72
"...................... MONTREAL	.51	.60	.60	.60	.69	.75		.75	2.07	.50	.50	.75
"........................ QUEBEC	.61	.72	.72	.72	.83	.89		.86	2.49	.51	.50	.89
"........................ TORONTO	.32	.38	.38	.38	.44	.50		.44	1.29	.49	.57	.50
NEW BRUNSWICK............. MONCTON	.66	.78	.78	.78	.89	.95		1.12	3.36	.89	.75	.95
NOVA SCOTIA................. HALIFAX	.66	.78	.78	.78	.89	.95		1.12	3.36	.89	.75	.95
MEXICO............ CITY OF MEXICO	2.68	.268	2.34	3.06	3.06	2.91		2.76	9.18	3.68	2.68	3.80
"............ TORREON, POTOSI	2.68	2.68	2.34	3.06	3.06	2.91		2.76	8.18	3.68	2.68	3.80
".......... SAN LUIS, PACHUCA	2.08	2.08	1.83	2.36	2.36	2.21		2.16	7.08	3.68	3.10	2.08
"................... MONTEREY	2.08	2.08	1.83	2.36	2.36	2.21		2.16	7.08	2.98	3.10	2.08
"......... GUAYMAS, MAZATLAN	2.87	2.92	2.32	3.32	3.37	3.00		3.25	9.99	3.25	3.75	2.97

(Column G: Rates quoted upon request)

Group

A Chairs.

B Beds, buffets, settees, davenports, fireless cookers, all tables except dining, extension and dressing tables.

C Dining extension tables, porch swings.

D Den couch, dressers, dressing table.

E Desks, book cases, book shelves, magazine rack, hall chest, hall mirror, hall clock, hall tree, screen, fern stand, foot stool, foot rest, umbrella stand, tabourette, cellarettes, mirrors, china closet.

F Lamps, clocks.

G Springs.

H Kitchen cabinets.

I Willow furniture.

J Vacuum cleaner.

K Rugs.

NOTE—Transportation companies require that the total freight charges on a single shipment shall not be less than a specified amount called the "minimum charge." For example, if the minimum charge to your station is 50 cents, and by reason of weight the total charge should be below this figure, you would be charged 50 cents, regardless of weight or classification.

How to Figure Freight Charges. By referring to the above TABLE OF RATES you will find the rate per Hundred Pounds to various shipping points on the different articles we are listing. To ascertain the freight charges to a certain point, multiply the rate by the weight of the article given in the catalog description. For instance, we will say you live in Cincinnati, Ohio and you desire to purchase our Davenport No. 6 on Page 5. The shipping weight is 240 lbs. and by referring to the Classification list you will find davenports go under class "B" and in the freight rate table, class "B" shows rate to Cincinnati, 37c—making the total freight charge 88c. While the above table may not give the rate to your exact locality, by reference to it you can approximately obtain your rate, by taking the rate per Hundred Pounds to the nearest point named, you will find the rate to your City is almost exactly the same.

Prepay Stations are Railway stations having no Agent to collect freight charges. We do not prepay charges unless full amount to cover same is included in the order. Prepaying duty charges is prohibited by law.

I N CONCLUSION, we wish to state that it is our desire to "Live and Let Live," and that no place in our catalog, printed matter or correspondence, have there appeared ambiguous insinuations regarding our competitors or their products.

OUR METHOD of increasing the demand for our furniture is by devoting our entire attention to producing the very best in quality, and, by extending to our customers fair and courteous treatment at all times.

SUCCESS IS THE ONLY TRUE TESTIMONIAL OF BUSINESS INTEGRITY

Our continued prosperity since organizing in 1901 and our growth from a capitalization of $6,000.00 to that of $400,000.00 in ten years is sufficient evidence that the QUALITY of our furniture and the SINCERITY of our guarantee are unquestionable.

THE Y. M. C. A., WOMEN'S LEAGUE, GOVERNMENT AND STATE INSTITUTIONS are among our many satisfied customers from whom we have received thousands of testimonial letters, a few of which we are printing for your information and respectfully refer you to the following letter received from the South Dakota State Hospital after the receipt of $1,703.25 worth of furniture.

Yankton, S. D.

Brooks Mfg. Co., Saginaw, Mich.

Gentlemen—I am delighted to report to you that the carload of K. D. furniture, more than 300 pieces, which we recently ordered from you for the furnishing of the new women's building at the State Hospital at this place, has all been unpacked and set up and it is not in the least an exaggeration to say that it has far surpassed our expectations. So far as I know there is not a defect in a single piece. It is massive, artistic, strong and the very finest quality of oak. The quarter sawed material is superbly beautiful. You may be sure that when we are in the market for more furniture, of this kind, you will hear from us.

Yours very truly,　　L. C. MEAD,

Supt. South Dakota State Hospital.

and again on August 5th, after receipt of another car load amounting to $2,714.75:

Yankton, S. D.

Brooks Mfg. Co., Saginaw, Mich.

Gentlemen—I have yours of August 1st.

I am glad to be able to inform you, however, that the furniture arrived in good shape, has all been put together and now in the paint shop being finished. It is fully as satisfactory as the former consignment and will add materially to the coziness and good cheer of the institution.

Yours very truly,　　L. C. MEAD,

Supt. South Dakota State Hospital.

Fort Terry, N. Y.

Brooks Mfg. Co., Saginaw, Mich.

Gentlemen—In March of this year, the recreation room of the 100th Company, Coast Artillery Corps, was equipped with Brooks furniture which was sent in a knock-down form. It was assembled, stained and polished by members of the Company. Owing to the hard wear and tear to which the furniture in a barracks used by 100 men is put I intended to replace from time to time broken pieces but have been agreeably surprised to find that every piece has held up. I believe that Brooks furniture is everything that it is represented and recommend it as being easily assembled, neat in appearance and durable

Yours very truly,　　THOS. O. HUMPHREYS,

1st Lieut. Coast Artillery Corps.

Tishomingo, Okla.

Brooks Mfg. Co., Saginaw, Mich.

Gentlemen—The goods you shipped me arrived all O. K., and were very satisfactory, and in every way exceeded my expectations, as they opened up strictly in first-class condition, and in every way were as represented. The lot purchased from you can not be duplicated here at any of the furniture dealers for double the amount they have cost me. Thanking you for your courteous treatment, I am,

Yours truly,　　HARRY D. WORKMAN.

Beaver Falls, Pa.

Brooks Mfg. Co., Saginaw, Mich.

Gentlemen—I received my table O. K. and found it superior to any one in the local stores here. I feel sure that I have saved 50 per cent. by purchasing from you. I feel perfectly satisfied with the table and have highly recommended you to my many friends.

Yours truly,　　C. C. SHERRY.

St. Louis, Mo.

Brooks Mfg. Co., Saginaw, Mich.

Gentlemen—Your library table received in A No. 1 order. A business man of this city advertises, "If I don't haul your trunks we both lose money." Now I'll just borrow his quotation and say: "If I don't buy your furniture we both lose money." Believe me, a satisfied customer.

Yours truly,　　WALTER COLE.

Our Knock-Down Boats

WE completely cover the small boat field with a line of well-designed modern pleasure boats, furnished either in the knock-down or completed form.

Anyone can put together our knock-down boats or build a boat from rough lumber, by using our exact size printed paper patterns and illustrated instruction sheets. We can sell you a boat for about one-third what a factory would charge. If you want to know how it can be done, send for our new catalog.

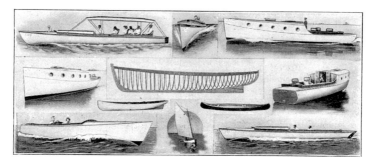

Our catalog shows a line of boats, each one embracing all the requirements of the thoroughly up-to-date pleasure boat—the result of twenty-three years experience in building and sailing boats—from a paddling canoe to a large cruiser.

Ten years ago we originated the pattern and knock-down system of boat building. It has revolutionized the boat building business.

Boats built by our system are now found in every civilized corner of the earth, and they have been built by amateurs at a saving of just about two-thirds of the cost if bought from a boat builder or factory.

Right now there are more boats being built by our system than in all the boat factories put together, and mostly by inexperienced men and boys.

Send for Our New Catalog

It quotes prices on knock-down frames, patterns, complete knock-down boats, motors, boat hardware and fittings, and completed boats ready to run.

We can supply you with the frame work for your boat, shaped and machined, every piece fitted, ready to put together, for less money than most lumber dealers would charge you for suitable rough lumber. (Patterns and instruction sheets to finish sent free with knock-down frames.)

We can save you (1) the boat builder's profit, (2) labor expense, (3) big selling expense, (4) seven-eighths the freight. **Figure it out yourself.**